Rainbows

NOTES

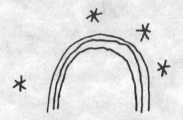

9   8   7   6   5   4   3   2   1
Digit on the right indicates the number of this printing.

ISBN 1–56138–693–6

Designed by Corinda J. Cook
Edited by Tara Ann McFadden
Printed in the United States

This book may be ordered by mail from the publisher.
Please add $1.00 for postage and handling.
But try your bookstore first!

Running Press Book Publishers
125 South Twenty-second Street
Philadelphia, Pennsylvania 19103–4399

Rainbows

NOTES

RUNNING PRESS
PHILADELPHIA • LONDON

It was on a rainbow that the gods of the North entered into their heaven; and it is at the end of the rainbow that there may be found the fabled pot of gold.

LOUIS UNTERMEYER (1885–1977)
AMERICAN POET

That gracious thing, made up of tears and light.

Samuel Taylor Coleridge (1772–1834)
English poet and critic

*L*ove's secrets, being mysterious, ever pertain to the transcendent and the infinite . . . and drop into us, as though pearls should drop from rainbows.

HERMAN MELVILLE (1819–1891)
AMERICAN WRITER

It is clear that two people, standing side by side admiring "the rainbow," are actually seeing light refracted and reflected by different sets of raindrops. Each person has his or her own personal rainbow.

Robert Greenler (b. 1929)
American professor

Hung on the shower that fronts the golden West,

The rainbow bursts like magic on mine eyes!

Charles Tennyson Turner (1808–1879)
English cleric and poet

. . . the colour gathered, mysteriously, from nowhere, it took

presence upon itself. . . . And the rainbow stood on the earth.

D. H. Lawrence (1885–1930)
English writer

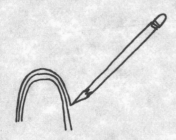

After a debauch of thunder-shower,

the weather takes the pledge and signs it with a rainbow.

Thomas Bailey Aldrich (1836–1907)
American writer and editor

If the sun comes out before the storm ends,

turn your back and look for a rainbow.

Rose Wyler
20th-century American writer

. . . the azure sky which, in just a few hours, would suddenly scowl with dark storm clouds, and then would cry warm, nourishing tears, and then, the tempest over, would smile again, the brilliant azure now gift-wrapped with rainbows.

Katherine Stone
20th-century American writer

So shines the setting sun on adverse skies, and paints a rainbow on the storm.

Isaac Watts (1674–1748)
English cleric and writer

The rainbow is a reflection of the light over the drops of water that react as if they were mirrors.

Aristotle (384–322 B.C.)
Greek philosopher

. . . a rainbow after a storm is the earth's aura, washed fresh and clean,

with all the beautiful colors set out for us to appreciate.

Crowned with the lovely rainbow, the world is in balance.

DINAH LOVETT
20TH-CENTURY AMERICAN WRITER

The ribbon nature puts on after washing her hair.

Ramón Gómez de la Serna (1888–1963)
Spanish writer

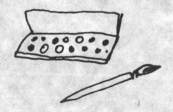

A rainbow painted on a thundercloud,

That faints away with the ascending sun.

FREDERICK TENNYSON (1807–1898)
ENGLISH POET

The true harvest of my daily life is somewhat as intangible and indescribable as the tints of morning or evening. It is a little star-dust caught, a segment of the rainbow which I have clutched.

Henry David Thoreau (1817–1862)
American writer

When it is dark the sun no longer shines,

but who can forget the colors of the rainbow?

S. G. Champion
20th-century English physician and writer

I always feel sorry for people who think more about a rainy day ahead than sunshine today.

RAE FOLEY (1900–1978)
AMERICAN WRITER

Too many people miss the silver lining because they're expecting gold.

Maurice Setter
20th-century American writer

The rainbow is . . . at the same time a bridge between the real and the unreal, the tangible and the intangible, the visible and the invisible, as well as a door that leads into the world of imagination and fairy tales.

Lama Anagarika Govinda
20th-century Tibetan Buddhist

The rainbow is the crossing point where whatever is human and divine meet.

It is a great dynamo where the energies of everything and everyone blend

and explode, creating new landscapes of joy and comprehension. . . .

Emilio Fiel
20th-century American writer

$\mathcal{T}$he rainbow, "the bridge of the gods,"

proved to be the bridge to our understanding of light—much more important.

ISAAC ASIMOV (1920–1992)
AMERICAN WRITER

A rainbow is for joy and promise. . . . It's a bridge to something wonderful. . . .

Phyllis Whitney (b. 1903)
American writer

The rainbow is only a manifestation of the unspoken. . . .

Dzeng Dharma Bodhi
20th-century Indian yogi

Heaven's promise in technicolor.

Anonymous

*"O*ne can enjoy a rainbow

without necessarily forgetting the forces that made it.

MARK TWAIN (1835–1910)
AMERICAN WRITER

Ground observers see only a portion of the rainbow. But most pilots have had the luck to look down and see the full circle that is every rainbow.

Carl A. Posey (b. 1933)
American writer

All the reds come first. Then the oranges.

Then the yellows. Then come the greens, blues, and purples.

She hangs her clothes in the same order as the rainbow.

R. L. Stine
20th-century American writer

. . . and filled the room with an atmosphere which made it seem like

living in a rainbow.

Candace Wheeler
20th-century American writer

The most beautiful thing we can experience is the mysterious.

ALBERT EINSTEIN (1879–1955)
GERMAN-BORN AMERICAN PHYSICIST

And, lo! in the dark east, expanded high,
The rainbow brightens to the setting Sun!

James Beattie (1735–1803)
Scottish poet

To hope and dream is not to ignore the practical.

It is to dress it in colors and rainbows.

ANNE WILSON SCHAEF (B.1934)
AMERICAN WRITER

Someday Jane shall Have,

she Hopes,

Rainbows for her Skipping Ropes.

Dorothy Aldis (1896–1966)
American writer

The sun athwart the cloud thought it no sin

To use my land to put his rainbows in.

Ralph Waldo Emerson (1803–1882)
English writer and poet

My heart leaps up when I behold

A rainbow in the sky!

William Wordsworth (1770–1850)
English poet

"A" rainbow is big enough for everyone to look at.

The rainbow is a sign of the unity among all people into one big family.

Eyes of the Fire
20th-century American activist

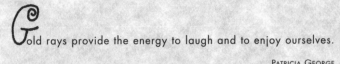

Gold rays provide the energy to laugh and to enjoy ourselves.

PATRICIA GEORGE
20TH-CENTURY AMERICAN WRITER

. . . may we be guided by the spirit of the rainbow,
toward harmony, cooperation, and respect for diversity.

Starhawk (b. 1951)
American writer

Like the rainbow, peace rests upon the earth. . . .

Edward George Bulwer-Lytton (1803–1873)
English writer and playwright